Becoming Coztototl

by

Carolina Hinojosa-Cisneros

flowersong BOOKS

Becoming Coztōtōtl

POEMS BY CAROLINA HINOJOSA-CISNEROS

FlowerSong Books
McAllen, Texas 78501

ISBN: 978-0-578-45506-8

Published by FlowerSong Books
in the United States of America.
www.flowersongbooks.com

Set in Adobe Garamond Pro

Cover painting by Jade Leyva
Cover design by Erasmo Cisneros
Typeset by Matthew Revert

“There are different kinds of spiritual gifts,

but the same Spirit is the source of them all.” – 1 Corinthians 12:4, NLT

Table of Contents

Acknowledgements

All my love and gratitude to the following publications for publishing these poems or some altered version of the poems.

SheLoves Magazine: "Testimonio of the Body"

The Acentos Review: "Fuga: Take Flight" and "Cantarito"

Bird's Thumb: "Madre"

The Rumpus: "Self-Portrait as Bone" and "The Unwelcome"

The Windward Review: "War Made Flesh" and "I Wish You"

Of note

"Blessed Be the Mother": lyrics from Cucurrucucú Paloma, Tomás Méndez, 1954

"Decolonial Cartography of the United States of America": América Invertida is a drawing by Joaquín Torres García

Blessing for Becoming Coztōtōtol

Beloved Yellow Bird,

I have felt a pride swelling since the day that I met you in my small apartment in East Dallas. With arms wide open I received you, a beautiful mujer bravely traveling towards freedom knowing the cost. You were just as beautiful to me then as you are now, a captivating reflection that eased my heart into admiration. We shared our stories that night, affirming each other's becoming. Recognizing each other's hungry spirits and beautiful brown skin, we decided then and there that we were sisters.

When you asked me to write a forward for this stunning collection of poetry it lovingly came to me in letter form. I believe it is because I want any person who might pick up this book to know that the beauty in these pages and the beauty that is you, is only birthed through the soulful work of relation. As indigenous mestiza women charged with the task of finding our way back home, relation is our greatest and often times most painful lesson, one that bleeds us with tenderness and humility.

I have been humbly sitting with your words for days now. I have felt the tenderness of my heart stir in mourning and celebration knowing your courageous testimonies are my testimonies and the testimonies of our women. I am moved by the spirit of your mothers and your children that rightfully take up space on these pages with such grace and respect. Their presence is so clearly the sacred earth that holds your fire, that holds my fire, that holds the fire of our people; lost tribes hungry to be led home. Coztōtōtl, mi querida hermana, your offering in these pages remind me, remind us, that the only sure way home is through love.

I am honored to watch you in flight.

With all my love and hunger,

Edyka Chilomé

"Blessed be

the mother who spreads her wings in resistance.

Blessed be

the mother who reclaims her land.

Blessed be

the mother who meets the devil nose to nose

until her hijitas and hijitos are returned to her."

For

Faith, Ryan, y Brooklyn

Bone of my bone

Carry our stories well

Becoming

Coztōtōtl,
como pájara alumbrada,
salgo de tu pecho roto.

In Lak'ech

Mi'ja, you are more than
shared flesh. You are
warrior at evening time.

You are powerful voice
at morning prayer. You are
ancestral lucha burning
sage under your bare feet.

Descalza, the earth ignites,
you into the day como Águila,
eagle spirit. Mi'ja, you are
of madre tierra. You are

trenzas por la madrugada.
Holy spirit ribbons through each
braid of charcoal. You are
curious fingers through carrot

strips. Orange fire in your mouth-
a dragon of giggles
where I find God
on a chipped tooth.

Coahuiltecan

I am from the spring, from
the grit in the nailbed
of my Mamá Grande's hands

I am from between syllables
American tongue can't unfold
Coztōtōtl-

Yellow bird perched on
willows that are despeinadas
like me at two years old—

que nudo es éste?
I am from where abuela slides
her pinky finger through straight

knots caked into threads of hair
from rolling too many pink foam rollers
because I wanted natural curls

not straight disasters
remolinos and tumbleweeds
piled like labor on my head

but abuela says, *es tu pelo liso,*
mi reina. Everyone wants your hair
like Sister Mary Alice.

I am from the Spring, from
the straight hair and nun envy,
from the grit of my beforemothers

Decolonial Cartography of the United States of America

I trace
my fingers
over the

equator

on the
mercator map.

I recall
the map—
América Invertida—

where the
north is not
pregnant
with empire,

where the
South is

Barefoot
Queen.

Testimonio of the Body

You, like a Jasper stone,
healer of duplicitous tongue.
Courageous salt deposit –
I find you unmoved, misshapen,
borrowed from familiar words.

Guided light, unmuted
beneath my Lazarus shroud.
Arisen from (d)(l)ust –
sins of my foremothers.

Spoken for, removed from implicit
layered tierra *firma*. Kneaded
bands of our stories smudged
clay soul. How, like Mary, we wept.

Hungry generational wound,
vigilant keeper of history, bold liar.
But in me, Imago Dei –
Thirst from wellspring.

My body, I aligned with you,
crowned with a thorned faith.
Heaven, open-mouthed, spoke,
"Fix your eyes in upward wonder."

You, like a Jasper stone,
nurturer of creative inner spirit.
Wise evening traveler –
I find you contemplative, subtle,
an accidental mulch.

Blessed Be the Mother

On holy land, between a mesquite shrub
and a Mexican willow whose purple buds bow
in adoration, a mother sets out on a pilgrimage,
un peregrinaje en el camino de una santa tierra.

She carries her child on her hip
like women have always carried this world,
ganchado – between the sacred bosom of life
and the warrior thigh that crushes the serpent.

Her talones kick up dirt, a holy danza amid
a swirling, languid breeze on land
which has been stolen from her.
Chin held high, wings spread wide,

she is the resistance.
She knows what awaits her arrival
at the border—el diablo anda suelto,
ready to rip the world from her hips,

but she knows where to hide the medicine,
tucked beneath her hijita's wings.

Cucurrucucú paloma
Cucurrucucú no llores

As hijitos and hijitas sit in manmade cages,
detentions they will call them, their wings carry
los antepasados like rayos de luz within.
And when the cage gets lonely, los antepasados

remind hijitas and hijitos of the land they stand on.

And they will hear

Cucurrucucú paloma
Cucurrucucú no llores

A mother's pilgrimage never ends.
She journeys the many separations
she's endured since giving birth to the world.
On holy land, between a tent city in Tornillo

and the lurking eyes of government institutions,
she prays her rosary, beads she must recall by faith
since their confiscation at port of entry.
She remembers the medicine she hid in the wings

of her hijitos and hijitas. She sings to herself

Cucurrucucú paloma
Cucurrucucú no llores

Blessed be
            the mother who spreads her wings in resistance.
Blessed be
            the mother who reclaims her land.
Blessed be
            the mother who meets the devil nose to nose
until her hijitas and hijitos are returned to her.

Bendita sea la madre.

On holy land, between a mesquite shrub
and a Mexican willow whose purple buds bow
in adoration, a mother sets out on a pilgrimage,
un peregrinaje en el camino de una santa tierra.

Leftover Olives

I ate leftover olives.

Mother used the oil
to swab
the bottom of my feet.

A resfrio cure- all.
Cures a cold
that jars
my chest, screams
into the air, dies
heaving brute lungs.

Wise medicine
tales from Ma Grande.

Mi'ja

My belly swells
my ombligo bulges – outie

Forests of lungs sprout
inside me, sparks of electricity
surge through tiny limbs
and chest walls

Umbilical bridge connects
                her body to mine

Placenta swishes and swashes -
an ocean of life
for a human I've yet to meet

Her huesitos harden
enough to carry our stories
our dichos, our chisme
our traditions

I will carry her through death y
bendiciones to pave a narrow path
where she will one day warrior on her own.

Our umbilical bridge severed yet revered.
She will wear papi's name until she finds her own
to wear like a revolution against us.

For mi'ja,
the life inside my body –
tierra   blessings   magic.

I pray her life be
more than flesh and hueso.

I pray her light and spirit carve rivers.
New life, bridges of hope.

Fiesta

I gather these moments,
string them together
like the papel picado in our living room,
festive, yet peckered nonetheless.

In America I am celebrated
for my ability to give birth,
but to keep my full-time job
I must be cut and shaped with precision,
hung in an office which holds cheap conversations.
The onlooker convinced
I am a beautiful piece of décor
to adorn the walls
on Cinco de Mayo.

Fuga: Take Flight

I can tell you what I'm not wearing.
The hand carved cedar rosary
my mother gifted to me on my twelfth birthday.

Grab from my neck a prayer bead
roll it between fingers, find nothing but sweaty collarbone.
            I will be caught and deported.

Nervously, I rummage through jean pockets
nearly melted from desert sun, finger
            my breast pocket marinated in dirt.

Sweat forms small blisters of lodo on my chest.
I want to Holy Mary my mother's rosary back into existence.
            Prayers   fall   around   like
                      bright   marbles of   misfortune.

Border patrol points me out from the brush.
  I   run.
My sister is on the other side of the border.
I continue to gallop forward.
Sin parar.

Gun drawn.

Tears, like rivers, carve their way down my face
through skin and earth.

A   shot   is   fired.

Tight chest.

Tattered fear hangs on barbed wire. I dive underneath.
        Throat becomes a hollow conduit.
        La migra steps behind me, another shot fired.
Dirt cuts eyes. Chest tight. Knees buckle.
        Body lunges forward. Hands reach toward the sky.
Face hits dirt, rocks lodge themselves
in my mouth, break teeth.
        Eagle lets out a cry that reminds me of our old house in San Antonio.

Al otro lado. Where we were Americans.
Warm chest mangles me. I will not survive.
        Border patrol plants knees near my head. A voice inaudible.

Shadow smothers me.

Vision excuses himself.

Air swells with
absence of
                                        sound.

Madre

The curve of my spine
hides beneath
brown speckled skin.
I find a tender nodule -
flesh - in battle
with pigment absent space.

Se pone de pie en guerra.
Spanish attempts to conquer
Arabic, a pressing of epidermis.
Porque somos Católicos.
Cupped abstraction
on my lower back.

Lone, raised pile of flesh
determined to claim stake.
Between my olive branch fingers,
I clip the brave avenger,
cause lightning pain
away from the bending.

Chamoy crimson puddle
e x t e n d s
its gratuitous hum
along the bridge of my vertebrae.

Self-Portrait as Bone

Broken in four places.

At the joint,
where Ma came home
with another man,
desperate for shade
of a family tree.

Under the marrow,
where my thighs
welcomed
a man
I did not want.

Between the cavity,
where the matriarch
pinched the eagle's beak,
abuela said, "Te lo dije.
Por andariega."

In the cartilage,
where I am mother
and stranger
both
the same.

The Unwelcome

Doubt chose the curtains,
undressed our home like
a carcass ready for burial.

I made love to doubt when
it left behind sinewy broken
hearted attempts. I drew a bath

without seafoam promise.

I let it choose canela in mami's
rice water. I stuck my dirty
tongue in doubt, offered it purple

pens to write my sorrows twice.
I grabbed its working hand,
kissed it like sudden death held

its lying gaze. I pierced its rib
cage, pulled a sacrament for my
wet bosom and sent it on its way.

Cantarito

Water tastes of clay,
        gritty tongue ignites
                memories of thirst.

She begged for rain,
        sat on mother's lap,
                empty clay jug.

The well underground
        tiny hands pull
                sun crisped rope.

Water filled buckets
        wind chapped lips;
                eager eyes witness

lips lick clay,
        inhale Water birth,
                exhale civilized nations,

villages fostered mothers,
        people brought forth,
                season of savage

beasts steal Water
        held for ransom
                well above ground,

strong hands lock
        Water filled towers
                for eager lips.

Chapped with witness,
her hands hold
the cantarito filled

with purchased water.
Gritty tongue ignites
memories of thirst.

War Made Flesh

Reckoning plagues hungry soul,

          d i s p (l a c e d)

                    family,
                    figures,
                    and lovers.

Armorless, wielded machete
          in soft eyes speak
          honest cries

like when Jesus looked on
          tear-pierced mother Mary.

Greater purpose
          woven in
                    baskets made ready
                                   for the labor.

Like when the pecan shellers won
          the battle
                    against unfair wages,

Emma Tenayuca
          recognized their worth.

                    When the war is over
take care of your own and to God the rest.

I Wish You

I wish you wholeness. I wish you life. I wish
you the gift of daybreak where the sun kisses
the horizon and never asks for anything in return.
I wish you embers that burn tiny holes on your
soul to let the light out. I wish you understanding in this
body and in the next. I wish you a
transformed life, a freedom uncaged, disruptive of the systemic
oppression visible in the folds of your skin, on the lapel
of your marginalized body. I wish you
light on the trail under your bare feet. I wish you breath
where you have been suffocated, ahogada,
callada, excavada. I wish you
vida abundante – medicina para tu corazón fiel.
I wish loyalty to your hands as you navigate words
and carry down history in the stream of your back, bone
of my bone. I wish you ease when you masticate
the gristle of family and faith.

Ma Forgets Coffee

If maybe I heard God in the nostril   cavity
that   held a   snore so deep my father
-in-law rattled   the Parkinson's right   out
of his hand   back to the   60's
when he   held   my   \\mother
-in-law   in the crook of his arm while
she\\   still   remembered

who he was. Back to a time when the cold
didn't confuse her like   boiling ice
drinking   sand in a mug that tastes
like the   coffee she\\   forgot to pour
into the cup   minus   water.

//Well, what's in it, Ma?//

Today \she\ shrugs, "Coffee." Because
coffee is the most \\   \\
familiar morning with   her   husband.
\\She thinks   she\\ made coffee like
the goddess in a nostril cavity that holds
deep snores, solemn   sleep where
no   one   imagines
there   is   no   \\cure.

Holy Is a Bird's Cry

Holy Spirit, can you hear?
Ashes of my (be)fore-mothers
vacillate over my limp body.

Temptation coils my throat.
Vexed desert sands, canyonous
t(r)eason is deft possibility.

Mirage of doubt pesters
like a fly buzzing at death.
I hear Mary

call my faith.
Mother, I do not pray anymore.

I feel the Jesus of my mother
cup the crane of my neck,

close his eyes over the kettle,

and blow medicine into the fold.
He brings his mouth to speak

but I have already fluttered away.

Mil Gracias

There are not enough thanks in the world that I can give to my community. Over and over we are medicine for each other. Comun-unidad, you are not afraid to give and to pour into those around you no matter the hour. May I be as loving and nurturing to those around me as you are, and have been, to me.

To God, Creator, Holy Spirit Mother, Jesus, the Blessed Virgincita, I am indebted to you until life is plucked from my chest to make way for new spirit and gentle wind.

ire'ne lara silva (Maestra) for a gentle nudge toward life.

Dr. Cantú for absolute wisdom in polishing this librito.

Dr. Quintanilla for apoyo.

Natalia Treviño for goddess eyes and sacred heart.

FlowerSong Books for giving my poems una casita con ustedes.

For Santa Fe Episcopal Church, house of flowers, poets, and scholars.
Jade Leyva for your kindness in allowing me use of the cover image. It is perfect as are all your paintings. Of the art: "*Loving Nature— "She is a child of the earth holding a precious bird with love; this behavior makes her royalty among nature and Earth gives her a flower crown"—painting, by Jade Leyva (https://squareup.com/store/jade-leyva-art).*

David Bowles for teaching us our language.

Laurie Ann Guerrero for naming me years ago.

The online communities of social media, where I have met hundreds of people who never tire in championing others. You know who you are. I am so grateful for you.

Erasmo, for understanding, patience, and respect. Tlazocamati huel miac. Te quiero mucho.

Tonantzin, Maquilxochitzin, Sor Juana Inés de la Cruz, Ada María Isasi-Díaz, Gloria Anzaldúa, blessed teachers.

Author Bio

Carolina Hinojosa-Cisneros is a Tejana poet and freelance writer. Her work centers on storytelling, faith, and Latinidad. She is Jack Sr. and Doris McCord Smothers scholar at Our Lady of the Lake University where she is in pursuit of an MA with emphases in literature, creative writing, and social justice.

41954007R00024

Made in the USA
San Bernardino, CA
06 July 2019